Blue Moon

Poems

Ted Olson

Iris Chapbook Series
Oak Ridge, Tennsscc

Copyright © 2025 by Ted Olson

All rights reserved. No portion of this book may be reproduced in any form or by any means, including electronic storage and retrieval systems, without explicit, prior written permission of the author, except for brief passages excerpted for review and critical purposes.

ISBN: 978-1-60454-514-2

Section Illustrations: NASA/Bill Dunford

Cover Source Photo: Kym MacKinnon

Book and Cover Design: Robert B. Cumming, Jr.

Iris Publishing Group, Inc.
www.irisbooks.com

Contents

Introduction: From a Distance • 5

I

Pioneers • 11
Phantoms • 12
Fate • 13
Just Like Us • 14
Son Of A Gun • 15
Unkind • 16
The Summer Of '74 • 17

II

Fair Game • 21
Not To Be • 22
Being On Earth • 23
Sandlot Jungle • 24
Transformed • 25
Cosmology • 26
Mantra • 27

III

Silent Night • 31
Gift • 32
Human Nature • 33
Home • 34
Framed • 35
Tornado • 36
Storm To Pass • 37

IV

Going Under • 41
Roadkill • 42
Bus Driver's Blues • 43
Unnoticed • 44
The Rest • 45
The Scientist • 46
Winter Solstice, 2020 • 47

V

Blue Moon • 51

From a Distance

In May 2009, the publisher of *Rapid River*—a monthly magazine distributed in and near Asheville, North Carolina (for free)—invited me to serve as the periodical's regular poetry columnist (for free). The offer surprised me because *Rapid River* covered the arts and culture scene in a city located 70 miles from where I resided (on top of Roan Mountain in East Tennessee). Although I had once worked as a Blue Ridge Parkway ranger, it had been 15 years since I had spent much time in western North Carolina. And I had never lived in Asheville.

Why was I selected for this role? Perhaps the publisher was aware of my 1998 study of western North Carolina's traditional culture *(Blue Ridge Folklife)*? I doubt that he had read my 2006 collection of poetry *(Breathing in Darkness)*—few copies ever circulated—but maybe he was aware of the anthology series I edited featuring new literary works by a range of authors *(CrossRoads: A Southern Culture Annual)*? I accepted the *Rapid River* role, assuming that through researching and writing such columns I might explore interrelationships between poetry and region. I sought to understand how poetry might most effectively express the "soul" of Appalachia, the region in which I (and most of those who might read my columns) lived.

In my columns, I investigated the ways that poets from Appalachia (and a few poets from other places around the world) balanced their artistic and spiritual aspirations with their regional identities. It was instructive to witness how poets improved upon the blank page (to paraphrase Argentine writer Jorge Luis Borges) in composing poems that evoked regional landscapes while invoking universal themes. I yearned to know how highly accomplished poets wrestled with craft in the effort to create poems that accurately and insightfully projected a "sense of place." And it was fascinating to learn how poets negotiate language (an artificial and sophisticated mode of communication) as well as poetic form in order to memorably and accessibly render their interpretations of the interrelationships between people and the natural world.

I had composed poems for decades without consciously committing to a specific set of poetic principles. Now, in the columns I wrote for *Rapid River*, I analyzed the perspectives of other poets and began to reexamine my own principles. I kept in mind that poetry—being the domain of human emotion—defies categorization and quantification and thus does not generate a "philosophy" in any structured sense. In poetry, "principles" are strategies for trying to harness feelings and thoughts in the hope of conjuring meaningful verbalized understandings from inherently elusive and complex human experience.

Those *Rapid River* columns prompted me to question my personal rationale for poetry. I realized that, while it may often be perceived as sacred, poetry is not sacrosanct. There is no sacrilege, I observed, in investigating the nature of poetry and in asking challenging questions of beloved or of brand-new poems.

A year into my stint as poetry columnist, I received my first correspondence from a *Rapid River* reader. Published writing can be an unintended monologue, so I appreciated the feedback. The writer of that letter, an activist based in Asheville, asserted that a poetry column serving this particular community ought to focus on issues of concern to working-class people. I thought then (as I think now) that advocating for social justice is one of the vital roles poetry can play...and can play well if that theme receives expression from a skilled poet. From my observation, though, poetry can suffer under the strain of seeking to be sociopolitically relevant. In my opinion, a poem is most likely to grow wings, aesthetically speaking, when freed from the need to be useful.

However, I, as a columnist for a popular periodical, recognized that one of my responsibilities was to respond to readers' opinions. In an October 2010 *Rapid River* column, I publicly thanked that letter-writer (without disclosing that person's identity) for sharing a valid viewpoint. Then I formulated a list of the principles that guided my reading of other people's poetry and that factored in my own poetry. Today, many years after it was sketched out, the list (shared below) still—at least to me—reflects a worthy perspective.

- Poetry helps the poet and, if a poem is effective, the reader to come to terms with the complexities in human experience, such as feelings, thoughts, ideas, and sensations.
- Poems can make connections between diametrically opposed forces and hence can forge a sense of order out of chaos.
- A poem can help the reader endure pain and frustration; that is, poetry can be manna for the spirit.
- A poem can take on an identity separate from the experience that "inspired" it.

- A poem reflecting greater loyalty to craft than to some deep human experience is likely to be rather lifeless and mechanical.
- In order to communicate directly and honestly with others, a poet should try to avoid language that is self-consciously smart, clever, and witty (in the socially refined, upwardly mobile sense of that word).
- Metaphors should be used sparingly in poetry—and only when they help illuminate a poem's theme.
- Rhymes, if utilized in a poem, should enhance that poem's musical structure, and should not be employed to create a pattern of predictable phrasing.

• • •

    That 2010 letter was the only *Rapid River*-related communication I would receive. By the summer of 2012, I decided that my usefulness as that periodical's poetry columnist had been exhausted. Other opportunities and responsibilities were waiting: my second book-length collection of poetry *(Revelations)* was about to be published, and I was committed to producing and curating several documentary albums of Appalachian music. It was time to move on—there was little more I could contribute to Asheville's artistic community from a distance.

    The poems in *Blue Moon* owe their existence—their form, their sense of place and purpose—to my three-year stint as a poetry advocate for a community in which I have never resided. I dedicate this collection of 29 previously unpublished poems to the poets (historical and living, regional and international) whose work inspired my *Rapid River* columns—and to all people who seek to understand the "soul" of Appalachia.

—Ted Olson,
January 2025

I

Pioneers

Seeing trees from here to the horizon,
our pioneers panicked, then gathered sticks
and fashioned makeshift castles. They survived,

slaughtering the beasts that foraged within
the forest, using bison bones as stakes
to prop up the crops they stole. So they thrived…

but all they left's a legacy of ghosts:
soulless houses and paved roads—our domain;
here we toil, raking leaves off a brown lawn.

This place seems dead, though sometimes at night hosts
of shadows—animated by the Moon—
rise up, loom over us. They're gone by dawn.

Phantoms

My wings torn, I fluttered in a whirlwind,
then woke up, my limbs sore. To the window
I staggered, struggling to see, as fog thinned,
colors swirling in the house's shadow:

there, defying the sky, were butterflies:
fritillary, swallowtail, monarch, queen.
I stood...wondering why our dreams are lies—
why we'll never be airborne on our own.

Fate

And what will be revealed? You'll see: morning
is imminent...yet surely not assured
now, it's true: between this and that moment
a nightmare might happen without warning—
your house disappearing (underinsured)
beneath a meteor; your body (spent
through work) worthless...your soul free, adorning
the dark like a bonfire flame, the stars blurred.
Just wait: your fate will soon be heaven-sent.

Just Like Us

Yearning to reinvent itself
our generation's erecting
its own monuments, rejecting
statues of those who lived before
that village became this city.

Some forebears squandered the world's wealth,
built mansions with guards by the door;
born to privilege, they preferred pain,
survived through subjugation, greed.

We may be the last to pity
and the first to condemn those souls,
yet they're here for *us*: still, their creed—

ignore parts when extolling wholes—
is ours. We can learn from their stain

on our landscape...lessons in stone.

Son Of A Gun

Play with that toy and
you'll regret the hour.
Grasp it in your hand:
you'll feel strange, power
pulsing in dead air.
Soon it may change course,
be your master. ...*There,
it controls the source.*

Unkind

If through persecution or fear
you raise your voice, your arms,
you'll be sacrificed, that's now clear:
God's unkind creed—who harms
others will live, though judged as cruel—
is their deed: your demise
is their muse. With faith as a tool
they'll craft their state of lies.
You, naturally selected
by accident of birth,
should know...you won't be protected
in their heaven-on-earth.

The Summer Of '74

I should have been fearful, bearing bad news
to neighbors in worsening Washington—
the headline warned, "The Wolf's at Our Doorsteps"—

but I did not see dangers or dark views;
I could not understand or care, back then,
about power, lies, the misdeeds of creeps;

I had a task: deliver black-and-white
scripts to believers and enact a myth—
a play for Truth, staged daily in their minds.

Newspapers, like the scrolls of yore, could right
wrongs, wake souls. I quit that job (my first) with
school's start…smarter, knowing how Act 1 ends.

II

Fair Game

Roaming at night alone, heading somewhere
down a dirt road, I heard something rustling—
crunching leaves, snapping twigs. I had to stop
there, needing to be certain it was air,
because if it wasn't a gust bustling
in woods but a bear against a backdrop
of darkness, this was fair game: quivering
child, animal aroused from winter rest.
Whatever it was, I was shivering,
exposed and afraid, so I ran away
from where I might be to what I knew best,
my senses and mind unwilling to play.

Not To Be

Just logged, this place was—remains—harsh:
I'm trudging through a frozen marsh
with uncertain motivation
toward a certain destination...

as when a child: I yearned to see
enormous moose rumored to be
sunning themselves here; I left camp
running, but soon my feet grew damp.

I turned back. Had I ventured forth
in that wilderness this far north
I'd have been savaged, I suppose,
by ticks, leeches, and mosquitoes.

Decades later, I curse the choice.
Surely a sadness in my voice
echoes the moment I surmised
dreams are not to be realized.

Being On Earth

Jumping from the lowest branch, he
picks up the stick he'll lean against.
Legs asleep, unused to walking,
he lumbers toward his destiny
across the field...there, he once winced
when he witnessed a cat stalking
a jay eating an acorn, not
looking; but the boy watched the lurch,
heard the shriek. Having learned to fear
being on Earth, he had long sought
to flee that curse, climbing to perch
in the oak's crown, to be as near
to the Sun as his own weak limbs
would permit. He was out of place
up there—a featherless biped,
exposed skin subject to the whims
of weather. Hobbling without grace
he'll look behind him and ahead.

Sandlot Jungle

The last time I was here
this was bare ground: no weeds,
no uncut wildflowers.
A random cloud drew near;
a pod spawned feathered seeds,
and sprouts followed showers
from soil roused by the Sun.
In time a vacant lot
became Rousseau's jungle,
the old order undone:
a warming climate brought
shrubs, then trees, a fungal
forest. I've returned where
with ragtag childhood friends
playing pick-up baseball
I swung madly at air...
a memory that ends
with a ball past the wall
rising. How it would land
no one wanted to know—
we all ran home. Word spread
that a marauding band
of apes smashed a window—
that when found they'll be dead...

Transformed

I lived in this town without fear or hope;
then at sunrise I awoke—heard laughter.
Looking out on a familiar landscape
transformed, I watched a dog with a sweater
lagging behind a man without a coat;
a woman slogging along in high heels;
a car skidding to miss a crossing cat;
kids sliding on sidewalks heading to schools.

It's odd to see my neighbors so surprised
by snow. We in the land of loblolly
shouldn't like these flakes—here, sameness is praised;
yet we yearn to be serious, silly,
spontaneous…to stop trying so hard
to remain on paths plowed to keep us safe.
With both fear and hope, this morning forward,
I'll move through life knee-deep in joy and grief.

Cosmology

Alarms have the power to set one free
from bad dreams. Clocks prompt one to don work clothes.
I once trusted such gadgets, but clearly
they're worthless for telling where the soul goes.

That story: night's purgatory; sunrise
draws up the shades. Then some chiming church bells
wake the town...and to me they sound like cries—
strangers trapped in timeless heavens and hells.

I find myself outside, thinking people
need to be rescued. Who am I judging?
Heading down the sidewalk toward the steeple,
neighbors nod my way, smiles never budging.

Is it communion or confrontation?
Though their cosmology baffles me so,
I follow that crowd, that congregation
inside, willing to learn what I don't know.

Mantra

Days are short. Night is long. That's what he thought—
or what he hoped we'd think he thought. In bed
I lay, just six, feeling sick—my body
stiff, mind stunned by the lesson I'd been taught,
his warning of where souls would go when dead.
His fiery sermon, bolstered with shoddy
logic, propped up his church's firmament;
biblical images inspired panic.
His voice cracked when judging souls unworthy
to be saved...unless we'd choose to repent
things we didn't do or say. His manic
argument, a monster unleashed, woke me.
It was first light, raining. I dressed for school,
and with my lunchbox, books, and umbrella
I stepped out, now believing, right or wrong,
I'd make my way alone, not be a fool
in someone else's story. My mantra
from then onward: *Night is short. Days are long.*

III

Silent Night

Here it is, evening:
we gave you our word,
you gave us silence;

there you are, leaving—
a migrating bird
without a conscience.

Here we are, waiting
in a world gone dark
for the Moon to show—

there it is, scraping
its flint edge, to spark
some fire on the snow.

Gift

Falling asleep
he had some doubt...
it was Christmas,
and at bedtime
he prayed, *Santa,
don't pass me by.*

When he awoke
the Sun was out;
a fleeting ray
filtered through grime
shone in his room:
a gift of sky.

Human Nature

Some birds gather things
that glitter—and display them.
We hide what we find.

Home

A beloved code-word
for all you can't have,
"home" lulls you backward
to where you can't live.

Made of more than wood
or brick or metal,
a home's neither good
nor detrimental:

your home's but a dream
you had once but lost
when thrust from the womb—
that comfort can't last.

In some house you'll die,
in a darkened room
with a worn-out sign
sighing "Home Sweet Home."

Framed

Lakefront cottage,
autumn evening:
a woman, framed
by shutters, leans
through her opened
window, waters
yellow flowers,
though no one else
will notice them.

Tornado

Some fear it's from hell,
some hope from heaven:

to us, skeptical,
it's a gust of wind—

it may peel away
our roof from our floor

but cannot sever
us, ever…even

when we're forced to flee
suddenly, we'll find

refuge together
in a ditch somewhere.

Storm To Pass

Snowdrifts from the sky
trap the doors, blocking
the path for walking:
you can't step that high;
but if you stay here
reasonably warm
and wait for the storm
to pass, *then* I'll clear.

IV

Going Under

After the storm she cried: "It's time
you ask for forgiveness. Start now
and maybe I'll remember how
to forgive, forgetting the crime."

His response: "I do understand
what I did and why it hurt, though
if you leave me, I fear I'll go
under...." Freezing, he squeezed her hand.

There was no electricity.
Sitting on the bed they gazed out,
First Quarter Moon bobbing about
like a bottle tossed in the sea.

It sank. His voice had disappeared.
With darkness prevailing, she stood
to leave the room, saying "It's good
to talk. Silence is what is weird."

Distracted, mesmerized by waves
crashing on rocks, he didn't hear
her last words, from the doorway: "Dear,
emotions aren't watery graves."

Roadkill

From her safe backseat perch
my granddaughter, in pain,
claimed we struck a fairy.
I couldn't see very
far because of hard rain,
but she was sure: "Stop! Search!"
she cried. I couldn't brake
or swerve to cross the line—
beside the road was mud—
so I replied, "No blood
in sight, everything's fine."
It wasn't a mistake.
Reacting fast to keep
the car from wrecking there
in fairyland, I lied—
something indeed had died.
She, not allowed to care,
would soon succumb to sleep.

Bus Driver's Blues

"The stars cannot shine
without the darkness"
is the sage advice
on that rusty sign.
Rarely a reckless
driver, I glance twice
(Free Will Baptist church,
New Age-sounding phrase),
begin to ponder:
*Why do these souls search
the world for God's praise?
Why do they wander
willfully from here,
fleeing by highway?
Hidden in plain view
is proof, loud and clear,
God has had His say;
I'll use my voice to
praise what's created—
the Universe, us—
as the fear of death
is unabated
for all on this bus...*
I take a deep breath,
focus on the road
ahead: I'll be there
for three winter nights;
I'll transport this load—
skiers—to fresh air
far from city lights.

Unnoticed

A man I don't know
falls behind the flow
of much younger feet
on a sun-drenched street,
unnoticed by most;
he, not quite a ghost,
shambles along there—
his old coat threadbare,
leather shoes untied.
With nowhere to hide
he stops by a store
that displays suits for
business and leisure,
leers with displeasure
through reflective glass:
that world, too, will pass,
he might be thinking…
*soon they'll be drinking
their failures away
as I did today.*
Not allowed inside
where others reside
he goes his own way
like a refugee—
condemned now to roam
in search of the home
he recalls knowing.
With shadows growing,
no doubt he'd embrace
some comfort someplace…

The Rest

In the shuttered coal town, the Sun
wakes what was left behind. His mind,
though, is like a snowbank, frozen,
embedded in a shut-down brain.

His old body, hidden under
a blanket, shudders in a space
darker than a shaft. He saw stars
once—they twinkled and fizzled out.

He's sleeping, as if his day's done.
Far from the rest of humankind
he thinks nothing of emotion,
being freed from pleasure, from pain...

but then he begins to wonder
why sunlight's caressing his face—
no longer can he see Earth's scars:
daffodils have begun to sprout.

The Scientist

After countless questions we still had to ask:
"Must we suffer so?" Nature's curt answer: "Yes."
You, deaf to doubt, heard "No" and took on the task
to save the species from a predestined mess.

Through painstaking experimentation and
a little luck, you fashioned the formula
that broke the code programmed by an unseen hand;
you flipped the future, using Death's spatula.

Winter Solstice, 2020

Sun's drifting off: Earth's imperiled, wobbling
like a top, spinning but slowing—a toy
in shaky hands. I drove up a mountain
to peer down at my town: a man's hobbling
in the dusk; streetlights flicker on; a boy
walks a dog beside a frozen fountain.
Most people are inside, shunning contact
or sick from the virus that took the world
species by species, body by body,
this year. Local folks first felt the impact
last spring, and many bedsheets were unfurled
by summer. Death became autumn's bounty.

Winter arrives with a cosmic surprise—
I search the sky and see it: one planet
(Jupiter) outflanking the position
of another (Saturn). To earthly eyes
those planets merge briefly after sunset
and glow as one orb. "The Great Conjunction"
hasn't occurred or inspired a witness
for centuries, said one astronomer.
We're still lucky, I believe, to be here—
wherever here may be—to behold *this*
conjunction in *this* dark year: Christmas star,
inextinguishable sparks of good cheer.

V

Blue Moon

I need to praise you, Moon.
Though you hardly exist—
no light or living thing
to thrill this crowded space—

I'm in awe. It has been
so long since we noticed
your rhythmic, revolving
beauty. You were the face

of mystery: remote,
changing. Men came to you
and took what they sought, left
trash; they never returned.

We yearn to sublimate
our earthly forms, but view
a reduced night, bereft
of dreams—streetlights have burned

deep craters in our minds.
Perhaps reflected rays
might inspire our tragic-
turned-comic consciousness

to heed Time's reprimands?
Meanwhile, I'll fix my eyes
and brain on your magic
rise from a cosmic mess.

Ted Olson has lived for many years in Appalachia, where he has worked as a naturalist, a park ranger, and a professor. His poems, articles, essays, encyclopedia entries, reviews, and oral histories have appeared in a wide variety of books and periodicals. Olson's poetry collections include *Breathing in Darkness: Poems* (2006) and *Revelations: Poems* (2012). Among his other publications are several scholarly books, including *Blue Ridge Folklife* (1998), *The Bristol Sessions: Writings About the Big Bang of Country Music* (2005), and *A Tennessee Folklore Sampler* (2009). He has edited books featuring literary works by James Still, Sarah Orne Jewett, Sherwood Anderson, and Cesare Pavese. Book series editor for the University of Tennessee Press's Charles K. Wolfe Music Series as well as associate editor and music section editor for the *Encyclopedia of Appalachia,* Olson is a Grammy-nominated record producer and album notes writer. Presently Professor of Appalachian Studies at East Tennessee State University, he served in 2008 as Fulbright Senior Scholar of American Studies in Barcelona, Spain.

www.ingramcontent.com/pod-product-compliance
Lightning Source LLC
Chambersburg PA
CBHW021001090426
42736CB00010B/1409